Two Isla
Two Couples,

Two
Camper Vans

A **NEW ZEALAND** TRAVEL ADVENTURE

JOANNE LYNN and **MARIAN KARPISEK**

Contents

Foreward

Reminiscing over photos and a dinner of New Zealand lamb chops a few months after returning from New Zealand, the memories rushed back. "Remember the day we discovered the penguins near the lighthouse?" "Watching the sun rise on the Matura River where we freedom camped was so awesome." "I'll never forget the magic of the glowworms!"

Suddenly we had a great idea. It would be fun to share what we learned with others who might want to do the same thing. Having started with no guidelines to help us, we think this book will give you a place to begin to fulfill your own dreams of a trip to New Zealand.

We had a wonderful time, planning and taking our trip of a lifetime, and now we are bringing those memories to life in these pages. We'll be sharing what we did and where we went, hoping that you, the reader, will enjoy our adventures and that our experiences and tips will be useful.

—Joanne and Marian

A Year of Planning

How did four California seniors come to be watching the sun rise over the banks of the Matura River in New Zealand, 7,000 miles from home? It all started at a women's social gathering in San Diego. Joanne and Marian were discussing travel plans when the question, "Where would you like to go next?" came up. It turned out that New Zealand was high on both our lists! Little did we know that we were embarking on a whole year of reading, planning, and preparation!

First, we needed to get our husbands on board as they had never even met. Then, once they agreed, we had to see if our dream trips would match up. Our goals initially were quite different. "Fishing," said Bob. "Jet boat ride," said Bill. "Hiking," said Joanne. "Learning about the Maori," said Marian. Four different ideas, but we all agreed that seeing the beauty and wonders of New Zealand was our top priority. And so our research began. With several guidebooks, the Internet, a travel agent, advice from friends, and many brochures, slowly we began putting our ideas together.

We used a travel agent because we felt overwhelmed knowing where to begin. She gave us ideas for what was possible and steered us in the right direction when we felt lost. Later on, she arranged for us to use our credit cards to pay for our vans in advance, saving us from paying in New Zealand dollars and incurring the attendant bank conversion fees.

Our first decision was figuring out how much we were financially comfortable spending and aligning our U.S. dollar budget with the exchange rate for the New Zealand dollar. Naively, we expected that prices for goods and services would be approximately the same or less, but we discovered that some things in New Zealand would be more expensive than we anticipated. Fortunately, we had allowed a higher bottom line than we originally expected to pay.

After our budget was established, the next consideration was how we wanted to travel. Cruise? Nice, but too long to get there and too short a time in each port. Guided tour by train or bus? Very complete, but too short. Car rental and hotels? Possibly. RV? Hmmmm, a definite possibility. All of us enjoy RV camping. The freedom to go at our own pace was appealing and we loved the idea of sleeping in our own beds each night. Not having to pack and unpack as we moved from place to place and stopping wherever we found something interesting made this option our ultimate choice.

The camper decision involved another series of meetings and emails. What size? What features? What amenities? Knowing that we would be driving on the left side of the road, we quickly decided we did not want a manual transmission that would require shifting with the left hand. This might not be an issue for younger drivers, but could be for us as we are all seniors!

With many RV rental agencies to choose from, we finally selected two *JUCY Condos* because they met our essential criteria; guaranteed automatic transmissions and porta-potties that could be used inside the van! We also appreciated that the van's smaller size would make driving on narrow roads and parking easier. We even liked the vans' bright green color that screamed, "Look out! Tourists on the road!"

Now that the van decision was made, there were still more things to consider. Would we limit our trip to New Zealand only? How long would we be gone? What time of year? Where would we start and end?

Visualizing ourselves snorkeling in clear warm water, we initially thought of including Fiji, Tahiti and Australia in addition to six weeks in New Zealand. Then reality set in. Looking at cost, potential weather, and how long we really wanted to be away, we scaled back our plans. Joanne and Bill would first snorkel for four days on Kauai with friends, while Marian and Bob would visit a nephew and his family in Melbourne, Australia. Then we would all meet up in Christchurch, New Zealand.

We decided to rent the camper vans for the New Zealand fall month of March, picking them up in Christchurch and returning them in Auckland. With travel time, including a day's layover in Honolulu each way, we would be gone from home for almost six weeks. We chose March because New Zealand schools are back in session, fewer people are on the road, and rivers are a bit lower making it a better time for trout fishing.

Once these major decisions were made, we booked our flights and reserved the vans. Whew! We sat back with relief, "We did it! We're on our way!" Then we realized there were some smaller, but essential, details we needed to address.

One consideration was whether to pre-book hotels and campgrounds. We decided to have our travel agent book our first night in a hotel close to the Christchurch airport. Through research on the Internet, we also booked our first campground near the *JUCY* rental agency. We reserved two nights just in case we might have questions about our campers. We also made our last night's campground reservation near the Auckland Airport so we would be sure to have a place to stay the night before we returned the vans.

After searching for additional campground information on-line and feeling inundated by all the information available, we decided that picking up lists from campgrounds once we were in New Zealand would be most effective. Campgrounds abound in New Zealand and we didn't need to know more before we arrived. This proved to be a good decision. If we had been traveling during the New Zealand summer, we would have made reservations ahead of time as campgrounds can get quite crowded at that time of year.

We then talked about maps, finding our way around, and communication. We bought a nice map at *AAA* and purchased a "New Zealand Adventure Travel Map" from *National Geographic*.

To navigate and save the cost of a rental GPS, we ordered a portable automobile GPS, with a map of New Zealand already on it, from *eBay*. For communication on the road, we decided to take along walkie-talkies, which proved to be extremely useful. We used them to signal each other when we needed to stop, explain upcoming turns, or point out a problem along the way. A bonus was commenting on the sights and making suggestions like "that's a beautiful beach, let's stop and take a walk!"

Next we had the cell phone and computer discussion. Marian and Bob had flip phones that they had unlocked before leaving the U.S. *AT&T* sent explicit instructions on how to do this. Buying New Zealand SIMs cards upon arrival in New Zealand would make the phones operational.

Joanne and Bill decided to buy an inexpensive pre-paid phone when they arrived in New Zealand and they found one at a shopping center in Christchurch. They also brought their smart phone with them to use as an additional GPS and map locator. They purchased an international package with extra memory that would facilitate this use. This did not work as well as hoped because we discovered there were breaks in reception while driving. We were extremely thankful for having had the foresight to buy the freestanding GPS and good paper maps.

We planned to use our tablets to keep in contact with family and friends at home. However, free Wi-Fi service was seldom available and service in some more remote locales was inconsistent. Campground fees for Wi-Fi also tended to be somewhat expensive, but e-mail still proved to be the best way to keep in touch.

Our final decision was how to handle money for day to day expenses. The Lynns chose to get New Zealand dollars from their bank before leaving home. The Karpiseks opted to get New Zealand dollars from ATMs, which turned out to be everywhere. We learned that credit cards can be used for almost all purchases, but it is necessary to have some New Zealand cash for incidentals.

What a process! Getting four people to agree to all of this! We were so excited when our plans were finalized and all we had left to do was figure out what to bring and how to pack. Bob brought his own fishing gear and we all made sure to pack for a variety of weather conditions and activities. We each had a small daypack to use on walks and one mid-size suitcase. (In retrospect, wheeled duffel bags might have been a better choice than the suitcases because they would collapse and take up less storage space.) After so many months of meetings, emails and phone calls, we were finally on our way!

Tips

- Visas to enter New Zealand are not required for U.S. citizens; check to make sure this policy is still in effect. If Australia is on your itinerary, you will need a visa for it.

- Tourists may not enter New Zealand with a one-way ticket. You must show a ticket for leaving the country.

- International drivers' licenses are not needed for New Zealand. Your current license from the States is good. If you're going to drive in Australia as well, check because International licenses may be required.

- Many large RVs are available for rent, but if you are not skilled in driving on the left side of the road, consider the fact that a smaller sized unit will be easier to handle. Also, many New Zealand roads are quite narrow and have small shoulders.

- Be sure you are guaranteed automatic transmission for your camper if this is what you want.

- Check to see if your rental agency allows pick up and drop off in different cities for no extra charge.

- Buy the most comprehensive insurance coverage offered by the camper van rental company for your peace of mind.

- Obtain a New Zealand GPS, either by purchasing one or renting one from the camper agency.

- A New Zealand adapter is necessary for charging any electrical items you are bringing from the United States.

- Decide how you will communicate with each other and with people at home.

- Customs officials did not seem concerned about small sized fishing flies in carry-on luggage, but check ahead for current status.

- Large fishing lures with hooks must go into checked luggage.

- Make sure fishing boots do not have felt soles and that the soles of fishing and hiking boots are clean. These will probably be checked by customs officials when entering New Zealand and on return to the U.S.

- Check with your medical insurance company to see if you are covered while you are in New Zealand.

- *Visa* and *MasterCard* are the most widely accepted credit cards.

- Check to see which New Zealand bank(s) are affiliated with your debit card.

- Off-season travel means fewer tourists, campers, and crowds.

We Set Off on Our Great Adventure

CHRISTCHURCH

Our year of preparation came to fruition and we were finally embarking on our long-awaited journey. As our plane began its descent into Christchurch, we excitedly strained to take in all we could of the New Zealand landscape. Rolling green hills with grazing cattle and small villages dotted the South Island, beckoning us to come explore. Near the airport, sunny skies gave way to a layer of clouds that obscured our view as we prepared to land.

We had booked rooms at the *Sudima Hotel*, located only minutes from the airport. After clearing customs, we called for the free shuttle. The weather had become windy and cold and we were grateful for a warm room and a restaurant where we could eat without having to go out into the rain.

During the night, the wind increased in intensity, rain began to pound down, and we woke to the worst storm Christchurch had seen in seventy-five years! We fervently hoped this was not a harbinger of things to come. However, this was the day we were to get our camper vans and nothing could take away that excitement.

After breakfast, we called the *JUCY* rental agency, just blocks away, and a van picked us up at the hotel. The paperwork went swiftly and easily and, before we knew it, we had obtained our campers and were being instructed in all we needed to know about driving and living in them.

The vans were small, but completely self-contained. By setting up a folding table, the "living room" transformed into a "dining room". At night, by rearranging the seat cushions, it morphed into the "bedroom."

The kitchen was fully outfitted with a two-burner gas stove, a sink with running water, a propane refrigerator, and a cabinet with tableware and pots and pans. At night, the kitchen doubled as the "bathroom" when we moved the porta-potty from its storage niche into the aisle. Net bags on the side walls of the van provided space to stow items frequently used, a roomy compartment under the "sofa" seat was perfect for clothes, shoes, and bedding, while the overhead bunk was useful for storing our suitcases and other items.

At last, keys in hand, we were ready to hit the road. Our first foray was onto the small, quiet street that ran between the rental agency and the hotel. We gathered up our belongings from the hotel, took deep breaths, and prepared to tackle the main streets of Christchurch.

Like children trying out new bicycles, Bob and Bill drove our camper vans carefully out into traffic. Everything felt different because we were driving on the "other" side of the road. Just as the guys were starting to feel a little confident, we encountered our first roundabout and intense concentration was needed. "Go left! Stay left! Look right!" we repeated over and over as we managed to navigate safely around each one.

Thankfully, we quickly arrived at our campground, *219 on Johns Motel*

& Holiday Park, chosen for being just ten minutes from the airport. We pulled in with a sigh of relief. The first order of business was organizing our campers and we began to "play house," unpacking and putting away our luggage. It was tight, but eventually we got everything out of sight. Next, we examined the accouterments that came with our campers. "There's everything we need and more! A toaster, a tea kettle, a heater and even real glasses!"

The one thing our camper didn't provide was a coffee pot so that was high on our list of "must haves" as we shopped at the nearby supermarket. We stocked up on supplies and groceries and happily found an inexpensive French press that would fill our coffee needs.

That night we had our first dinner in the camper— rotisserie chicken and a variety of salads. By the time we finished dinner, we were tired and ready to go to sleep in our "new homes." Making the queen-sized beds took a little

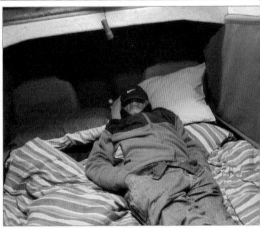

patience as we figured out how to stuff the duvets, but we soon wrestled them into shape and crawled into bed, lulled to sleep by the rain and wind.

Since it was still raining the next morning, we wanted to do something that would not involve getting too wet or take us too far afield. The *International Antarctic Centre*, located very close to the Christchurch airport, was the perfect place. Christchurch is the supply base for expeditions to Antarctica. The Centre is designed to let visitors get a sense of Antarctic life in a realistic setting that duplicates the frigid conditions as closely as possible. Participating in interactive exhibits, taking a 4-D Antarctic cruise, experiencing a simulated storm with snow and ice, and watching the little blue penguins waddle around was entertaining and educational. This taste of the challenging Antarctic environment is probably as close to the real thing as we will ever get.

Leaving the Antarctic behind, we braved the real winds and rain to return to the shopping center to buy a few more things for our vans. We discovered another "must have" was a doormat to keep dirt and mud from being tracked inside. A small rug for inside made our "living room" more cozy. We purchased these additional items at a thrift store and, for a small outlay of money, made our campers a little more homelike.

The storm had moved out by the next morning, so we opted to go into the center city to see the extensive damage done by the earthquakes of 2010 and 2011. Our GPS got us into downtown, but we discovered that it didn't reflect street closures. "Turn left at the next intersection" the GPS commanded, but "left" was nothing more than construction materials piled in the middle of the street! After a few false turns, we finally reached the town center and parked the vans.

As we had allowed a half-day, we decided that the double-decker *Hassel-free Christchurch Sightseeing Tour Bus* would give us an overview. This proved to be an excellent decision, as we viewed many parts of the city and saw for ourselves the horrible damage caused by the earthquakes.

Although some of the center city still resembles a war zone, it is evident that much rebuilding is occurring, with cranes and shipping containers everywhere. In one section, these containers have been repurposed to create a shopping center, complete with stores and even a bank.

Walking through the *Christchurch Botanic Gardens* and along the Avon River, created a tranquil feeling, far removed from the devastation of the city itself. Initially, we planned to go punting on the river, a popular activity, but the clearing weather made us anxious to be on our way.

Leaving Christchurch behind, we merged into the light traffic headed toward Akaroa. Although still novices, the guys were becoming more secure in the operation of the vans and felt comfortable driving along the highway.

Tips

- Check your camper before leaving the rental lot to make sure you have all necessary equipment and understand how to use it.

- Spend your first night camping near the rental agency.

- Make a reservation for your first night to alleviate concerns and make your arrival easier.

- Be prepared for road closures and construction in Christchurch.

- Thrift stores are a good place to purchase useful items that will make you more comfortable, but that you might not want to take home.

Basking in the Sunshine

AKAROA

Most traditional tours of the South Island do not include Akaroa, although it is a designated port for cruise ships. We included it in our itinerary on the recommendation of a friend who had recently visited there. She enthusiastically described its beauty and inspired us to make it our first stop out of Christchurch.

Route 75 was wide and traffic minimal, which made it easier to continue learning a new way of driving. The walkie-talkies helped us keep in touch even when we were out of sight of each other. However, as we neared Akaroa, the road became twisty with steep drop-offs and, in several places, crews were removing mudslide debris caused by the heavy rains. All of a sudden, the guys' driving skills were being put to the test. Glimpsing the harbor and knowing that we were almost there was a relief.

Parking our campers on the hill of the *Akaroa Top 10 Holiday Park*, we stared in awe at the picturesque harbor. Boats, bobbing at anchor on the shimmering blue water, took our breath away. It was getting late in the day so shopping for dinner was essential. Spotting the butcher shop, Bob and Bill went in search of New Zealand lamb chops while we went to the small, but diverse, grocery store to do the rest of the shopping.

Back at the campground, we discovered a wonderful amenity that we hadn't noticed in Christchurch because the torrential rains kept us confined to our vans. Each New Zealand campground has a kitchen building available to all campers at no additional charge. Inside are numerous stoves, microwave ovens, sinks, tables, and even a boiling water dispenser. Outside are barbeque grills and picnic areas.

It was much easier for our group of four to cook and eat dinner in the communal kitchen rather than in our vans. The kitchens often provided larger pots and pans, the generous space made meal preparation easier, and our vans stayed cleaner when we did not cook in them. Using the kitchen was also fun because we met fellow campers from around the world and exchanged information.

The kitchens, especially those near airports, offer another bonus. When campers are preparing to return home, they put their extra food and items they do not want to carry with them into a bin for others to take as needed. We scored big when we found an almost full bottle of olive oil, some "interesting" vegetables that we didn't recognize and, best of all, two camp chairs.

The next morning offered a perfect start to a lovely, lazy day, enjoying the view, and reveling in the fact that we did not have to drive anywhere. We wiled away the hours soaking up the warm sun that was so welcome after the rainy start of our trip. After lunch, we walked into town. Seeing a harbor excursion boat arriving at the dock, Joanne became excited about taking a nature cruise out into the ocean to see seals and dolphins, and she hurried to buy a ticket.

The rest of us were more inclined to stay on land so we said goodbye to Joanne and headed for the *Giant's House*. This unique garden, located just off

the main street, features an old house with a gallery of original artworks and terraced grounds filled with eclectic mosaic art forms. We were astonished as each turn on the garden path revealed a new and unusual sculpture. This is art meant to be touched, sat on, and appreciated up close and personal.

We were fortunate to discover the artist, Josie Martin, filling in for the ticket seller at the gate as we were leaving and we had an intriguing conversation with her. Walking down the steep hill from the house and back to the main street, we marveled at all we had seen.

Meanwhile, Joanne enjoyed her voyage out to the ocean. Watching seal pups swim in tidal pools in the rocks, seeing the waves break at the entrance to the harbor, and observing a small penguin fishing for its meal made this an enchanting day on the sparkling waters. Because no dolphins were seen, though promised by the brochure, the captain offered everyone a free ticket to try again the next day. Unfortunately, we planned to leave in the morning so Joanne wasn't able to take advantage of this offer.

Our dinner conversation that night was lively as we recounted our day. By the time the dishes were done, we were ready to retreat to our vans and snuggle into our own comfortable beds.

Tips

- Check out the kitchen at your first campground for "free" goodies left by departing campers.

- Look for camping brochures and tourist information at campground offices.

- Obtain camp chairs from your rental agency, or buy them in a larger city, as this will allow you to spend more time outdoors comfortably.

Our Road of Discoveries

AKAROA TO OTAGO PENINSULA

After consulting our maps and guidebooks over morning coffee, we set our course for the south, toward the town of Timaru. We estimated it would take about three to four hours to get there. As we were still not used to driving on the left side, the rural two-lane roads remained intimidating. Luckily, though, these agricultural areas and small communities were not heavily trafficked.

We stopped by a river access spot for lunch and appreciated the opportunity to get out, stretch our legs, and take our eyes off the road. Soon after lunch, we merged onto Route 1 with two lanes moving in each direction! This was much less stressful and we could relax and enjoy the scenery. Reaching Timaru, we headed straight for the *Top 10 Holiday Park*.

On our first foray into Timaru, we walked along the jetty of Caroline Bay. It was Saturday and sail-boats, tacking in the brisk wind, caught our atten-tion. We stopped to watch members of the local sail-ing club land their boats and winch them onto trailers and out of the

water. We also saw a sign indicating that blue penguins nest here, returning at night after their day of fishing at sea. We made a mental note to find out more and return in the evening.

We needed to go to the supermarket again and looked forward to browsing the wide array of foods available. Food shopping was time-consuming, but an enjoyable part of our routine. The stores themselves were not that different from those we shopped in at home, but it was fun to decide what new items to try and to figure out the quantities we needed by converting grams to ounces.

Acting upon advice from our campground host, we headed back to the jetty at 8 p.m. where we, along with a growing number of others, mostly locals, waited and watched eagerly for the little penguins to return. It was the end of the season and we were told there might not be too many. We did find one small penguin, hidden in the rocks, but none appeared from the sea. By 9:30, we were tired and, when someone told us the penguins might not arrive until midnight, we decided to call it a day. Still, it was a fun evening for all of us.

Rain poured down as we emerged from our campers the next morning. After making a mad dash to the showers, we gathered in the warm kitchen to review our maps and make the day's plans. We decided that the *Te Ana Maori Rock Art Centre* in Timaru was the perfect venue for this dismal day and we set off to find it.

Our young Maori guide, sporting tattoos that we discovered had great significance, gave us an informative tour. We made etchings of some rock art casts and expressed our interest in the petroglyphs. Our guide told us that the original rock art was located a short drive away. We couldn't pass up this opportunity, especially since the rain had stopped.

With a map from the Centre, we headed out of town on Route 82. Parking just off the road, we climbed a short, but steep, path to the alcove where the drawings remain, protected by a chain link fence. Although we were disappointed not to get closer, we were able to take pictures by aiming our cameras through the spaces in the wires.

Descending, we were awed by the magnificent view of the countryside and the distant mountains visible from this high point. We were definitely off the beaten track as there were no other people, or even vehicles, in sight.

Leaving the petroglyphs, we turned the corner onto Route 83, Sandal Road, and discovered *Elephant Rocks*. We were impressed by how much the

limestone rocks really look like elephants! As we walked among them, the sheep grazing on the lush grass seemed oblivious to us.

We continued on Route 83 back to Route 1, driving south along the coast. We had no clear idea how far we would go until we read in our guidebooks about the Moeraki rocks. These large, round, and smooth

grey balls can be seen along Koekohe Beach in Moeraki. Maori legends tell of a large sailing canoe shipwrecked along the coast. The boulders are the remains of eel baskets from the ship that washed ashore.

As this sounded interesting, we turned off the road and into the little community of Moeraki to

the *Moeraki Village Holiday Park.* We were intrigued when our camp hosts suggested we might like to eat at the local fish restaurant, *Fleurs Place.* When they offered to make dinner reservations for us, we thought "why not?"

Wending our way along the trail around the charming cove where fishing boats bobbed at anchor and houses nestled in the green hills above, we soon arrived at *Fleurs Place.* The food was creatively presented and delicious, the ambiance was delightful, and Fleur herself came over to talk with us. Later, reading the book, *Fleurs Place,* by Paul Sorrel, we learned that this restaurent is one of the most famous in New Zealand!

The next morning, while talking to some young Germans driving a *JUCY Condo* just like ours, we heard about a penguin hospital at the nearby lighthouse. None of our guidebooks mentioned this, but we thought it sounded fascinating. After meandering a bit over dirt roads running between sheep-filled fields, we unexpectedly came to a beach with huge piles of seaweed. We were strolling along the shore when a nearby pile suddenly moved. What looked like a deserted beach turned out to be a haven for sea lions basking in the sun on their seaweed cushions!

After finally stopping to ask for directions, we found the lighthouse where the penguin hospital supposedly was located. The lighthouse was closed and we were unable to find the hospital, but instead followed a path into *Kaitiki Point Wildlife Sanctuary*. There we found yellow-eyed penguins in their natural habitat. We stood spellbound by this serendipitous turn of events.

As we reluctantly tore ourselves away, we all agreed that these past two days of discovering things not in our guidebooks were among the highlights of our trip so far. And even though we never did get to the beach to see the Moeraki rocks, we did see several boulders in front of individual homes.

Continuing south through Dunedin, we threaded our way through narrow streets clogged with university students and uniform-clad children. Passing the imposing gothic-style university, we aimed our vans toward the Otago Peninsula and the *Portobello Village Holiday Park*.

After a short rest, we drove to the far end of the peninsula and the *Royal Albatross Centre*. This is the only place in the world where albatross nest on a mainland. Looking through binoculars, we watched several chicks in their nests and saw two of the adult birds take off and fly over the water. Although this was not the season for seeing large flocks, we learned a lot. We got an idea of how big and heavy these birds are by holding stuffed replicas of eggs and birds. It is really amazing that albatross can fly or even get off the ground!

Tips

- Talk to local residents, museum guides, and other tourists to find interesting places off the beaten track.

- Allow flexibility in your travel plans so you can change your itinerary if something new sounds exciting.

- We recommend *Fleurs Place* for great seafood and a delightful experience.

- Grocery shopping can be fun if you look for new and different local food items that we do not have in the U.S.

- Be sure to factor into your plans the necessities of shopping, laundry and other housekeeping chores.

Fishing, Anyone?

OTAGO PENINSULA TO TE ANAU

Leaving the Otago Peninsula behind, we started toward Milford Sound. Although we knew there were many places to visit in the southernmost reaches of the South Island, we chose to bypass them. Even with a full month to explore New Zealand, we couldn't see and do everything.

Gore, the brown trout capital of the world, was a "must see" for Bob. We couldn't miss it when we rounded a bend in the road and the huge brown trout sculpture that represents Gore's claim to fame loomed ahead of us. After posing for pictures in front of the trout and enjoying a picnic in the park, Bob walked across the street to a sporting goods store, where he bought his fishing license and talked angling with the owner. This chat elicited a recommendation that he should fish the Matura River, located off the Queenstown Road. Armed with directions, Bob was excited about wetting a fly and trying his luck for one of New Zealand's legendary brown trout.

While Bob gathered information about fishing and camping, the rest of us were successful in our thrift store search for two additional camp chairs. As a result, we now had four chairs, in varying states of repair, ready for our use

Jumping back into our vans, we found Highway 6, that leads to Parawa, where we veered off on a dirt road. Although this is private land, fishing and "freedom camping" are allowed in some places. "Freedom camping," a valued New Zealand tradition, means camping at no cost in out-of-the-way locations. This has caused problems at times for local residents and the practice is not wholeheartedly endorsed. Care must be taken to observe the guidelines and practice responsible stewardship of the land.

There were several sites that allowed fishing access, but many were not suitable for camping. We finally found a lovely meadow that was posted for camping and looked perfect, but we drove the short distance to the end of the road just to be sure this was our ideal spot. It was and we drove carefully across the field to park near the river.

The minute we stopped, Bob grabbed his fishing gear and enthusiastically hit the stream. The rest of us put our chairs by the river and sat down to enjoy the utter tranquility. (In all the time we were in our "private" campground, we saw only two other vehicles.) We felt like we were in the

heart of authentic New Zealand. Unfortunately the fish weren't biting, but Bob reveled in the opportunity anyway. After a late dinner and some more time by the river's edge, we crawled into our beds, lulled to sleep by the gurgling water.

Morning dawned with a brilliant pink and blue sunrise seen through the mist rising off the river. Life doesn't get any better than savoring a hot cup of coffee in the cool morning air, watching a variety of birds swoop and soar on the air currents, and feeling at peace in this very special place.

But now it was time to pack up our vans and return to civilization. The road to Te Anau beckoned and we had more adventures to pursue. Reaching *Te Anau Top 10 Holiday Park* in the late afternoon, we felt lucky to get side-by-side campsites.

The campground was across the street from an inviting walking path along the lake and we went out to see the sunset. Joanne stopped in town to check hiking options. Unable to rationalize the high cost of a guided four-day Milford Track walk, she and Bill settled for making reservations to go on a day trip.

Tips

- The best place to purchase a fishing license is at a local sporting goods store. Employees in these stores are extremely helpful in identifying local waters that are open to fishing, flies that are working at that time of year, and local guides who know the locale well.

- If you "freedom camp," know the rules and be sure to leave your camp as pristine as you find it.

- Buy something at a local shop and ask the shopkeeper for information on places of interest.

- If you need to charge electrical devices, official campgrounds with plug-ins are necessary at least every few days.

Fjordland: Quintessential New Zealand

TE ANAU TO QUEENSTOWN
The Lynns' Milford Track Hike

BY JOANNE

Waking to a cloudy day, Bill and I set off early in the morning for a guided hiking tour on the Milford Track with *Real Journeys*. The Milford Track is one of the most famous hiking trails in New Zealand and was on our "must see and do" list. After a bus ride and a one hour boat trip across Te Anau Lake, we reached the beginning of the Track. Putting on our rain gear, we started

hiking in a light drizzle along a wet path through rainforest, enjoying the feel of spongy moss beneath our feet. A little bird patiently waited for our footsteps to uncover some delectable morsel in the wet ground.

After enjoying lunch at the comfortable trekker's lodge, the *Glade House*, we donned rain gear again to venture deeper into the rainforest. Crossing a suspension bridge, we followed the trail for several miles along the clear Clinton River. Peering into quiet pools, we watched large trout swim idly, but there was no fisherman in sight. Bob would have drooled over this!

When the clouds unexpectedly lifted, we glimpsed waterfalls cascading down the high rock walls. With more than 200 days of rain a year (it's a rainforest after all!!) it was lush, green and a treat to walk in, but it was nice to know we would return to our warm, dry camper that evening.

The storm dissipated as our boat made its return journey across the lake and we were treated to a spectacular rainbow. Although it is possible to walk this trail without a guide, we were quite pleased with our tour. We thought it was worth the cost as we were able to see and learn so much and came away with a good idea of what a trek along the entire track would be.

The Karpiseks' Drive to Milford Sound

BY MARIAN

Bob and I decided to drive to Milford Sound to scope it out before our cruise the next day. As we pulled out of the Te Anau campground, a few raindrops fell and we wondered if this was the storm that the weather reports had predicted.

A stop for lunch at *Mirror Lakes* coincided with a break in the rain. Although the day was cloudy and reflections were not crystal clear, the twenty minute walk was well worth our time. The trail was flat and walking was easy. We barely got back to the van when the skies opened up once again.

Reaching the *Eglinton Valley*, we looked breathlessly at spectacular waterfalls cascading from steep rock walls. Pictures cannot convey the beauty and delicacy of these falls that graced the face of every mountainside into Milford Sound. What luck to have a rainy day, after all!

We reached the *Homer Tunnel*, a signal that the road to Milford Sound was almost at an end. This tunnel, begun in 1935, took eighteen years to complete and made it possible to drive from Te Anau to Milford Sound. The 3/4-mile tunnel is narrow, but large enough for two lanes of vehicles to pass each other carefully.

Arriving at Milford Sound, the sun suddenly peeked from behind the clouds and the waterfalls quickly began drying up. Strolling along the waterfront to the boat dock gave us an overview and, not seeing any sign of a campground where we could spend the night, we decided to check at the Information Centre. Unfortunately, there is no

longer provision for camping at the *Milford Sound Lodge*, but despite signs that command "No Overnight Camping," we were told that it is permissible to stay overnight in the car park in a self-contained van.

The car park slowly emptied and by evening there were only four campers left, three of them identical *JUCY*s! Dinner at the *Blue Duck Cafe*, with excellent food served in a stunning setting, made the evening delightful.

Although the humans had mostly left the car park, unfortunately the sandflies had not. A type of black fly, female sandflies are vicious and their bite leaves welts that itch and hurt at the same time. As fast as we killed them, more took their place. "Freedom camping" this time came with a definite drawback! It was not our most comfortable night, but by keeping ourselves totally covered, the sandflies did not have access to their meal (us!) and we managed to get some sleep.

Morning arrived with clouds hanging low and heavy over the Sound. However, as the sun rose higher in the sky, the moisture dissipated and the mountains emerged making this a postcard perfect view.

MILFORD SOUND AND THE RETURN TO TE ANAU

The four of us rendezvoused at noon and walked to the docks to get our tickets for the *JUCY* boat and a cruise of the Sound. As we were renting *JUCY* vehicles, two of our tickets (one for each camper van) were half price, a nice benefit.

Our boat's capacity was 200 passengers, but on this day there were only 50 on board. Although it was hard to believe, after the previous day's rain, the skies were clear and the water still and serene. In fact, the water was so calm that we cruised out into the Tasman Sea. The sparkling blue water and the lush green forests of the cliffs filled our senses with delight. We saw two exquisite waterfalls that flow regardless of the

weather and recent rainfall. It is easy to see why the Milford Sound is so highly recommended.

Leaving the waterfront, we drove back to Te Anau with a stop for a short, twenty minute, hike at *The Chasm*. Walking along a shady rainforest trail, the sound of rushing water filled our ears. We finally reached a bridge where we peered into the chasm and saw the water snaking its way down through the narrow passage. A well-fed kea and some parrots commanded our attention on the way out to the parking lot, adding some entertainment to this stop.

Returning to the same campground in Te Anau, we checked in and were relieved to settle down for a good night's sleep. Although there were still a few sandflies, they were not as prevalent as at Milford Sound. It was a lovely end to a fantastic day.

In the morning, we met for breakfast in the campground kitchen to discuss our day's plans. After much thought, we again decided to go in different directions for the day and meet up in Queenstown that night. The Lynns would take a glowworm cave tour and the Karpiseks would look for a stream where Bob could fish.

The Lynns' Glowworm Tour

BY JOANNE

While waiting to start on the Milford Track, Bill and I had watched a video of other tours that were offered and were captivated by the idea of going to see the glowworm cave. We walked back down the lakeshore to the *Real Journeys* headquarters, bought a pastry and coffee from a store nearby, and watched the ducks from a bench overlooking the lake while we waited to board our boat. The weather was calm and we enjoyed the thirty-minute journey to the cave dock where we met our guides.

First, we learned about the life cycle of the New Zealand glowworms. They are not really worms, but the larval stage of a fungus gnat that is similar to a mosquito. They build nests on cave roofs and string up to 70 connecting sticky threads with which to capture midges and other flying insects. The brighter the light, the hungrier the glowworm.

Our guide led us through narrow passages and along a subterranean river that twisted and dropped into pools. We loved this as much as the actual glowworm experience. Eventually, at the edge of a dark, water-filled cavern, we were helped into a small flat-bottomed boat. The guide pulled the boat along using overhead wires and propelled us into quiet waters. Looking up, we felt like we were viewing hundreds of bright stars all around. We sat quietly, taking in this amazing sight, as the boat slowly turned 360-degrees.

After the tour, we decided to continue exploring around Lake Te Anau, the largest of the southern New Zealand glacial lakes. We stopped at the *Fjordland National Park Visitor Centre*, checked out some trails, and discovered an inviting river that starts from the dam at the southern end of the lake. As we enjoy rafting and canoeing, checking out rivers is one of our favorite pastimes!

We reluctantly decided it was time to make a power run to Queenstown where we were meeting the Karpiseks. We had made reservations that morning, at the suggestion of the campground host in Te Anau, as Queenstown is popular and campgrounds there tend to fill up quickly. Also, a typhoon was predicted for the coast and people would be moving inland.

The Karpiseks' Travel to Queenstown
BY MARIAN

While the Lynns extended their stay in Fjordland, Bob and I decided to check out the fishing opportunities between Te Anau and Queenstown. The road followed Lake Wakatipu for many miles and the views of the surrounding mountains were stunning. However, there were no rivers where fishing looked feasible, and lake fishing, which Bob wasn't especially interested in, would have required a boat.

So, instead of stopping as we originally planned, we went directly to Queenstown and found our campground. Once there, we were thankful that we had taken the precaution of making reservations because it was full. We checked in and took advantage of the afternoon to stroll the waterfront and get a feel for the town.

When the Lynns arrived after dark, we compared activities and all agreed that Fjordland was one of the South Island's most spectacular regions. And Queenstown looked intriguing, even if there were lots of other tourists around!

Tips

- Feel free to go in different directions when traveling with others. All your time does not need to be together.

- A cell phone helps coordinate re-connecting.

- Make campground reservations a day or two in advance, even in the off season, for popular tourist destinations.

- Be aware that many tour buses drive the road to Milford Sound early in the morning and return in the afternoon.

- Rain gear is essential at all times of the year.

- Insect repellent for sandflies is advisable when you reach the west coast

It Takes More Than a Typhoon to Stop Us

QUEENSTOWN

The *Queenstown Top 10 Holiday Park Creeksyde* turned out to be one of the most unique campgrounds we have ever stayed in. It received *EarthCheck*'s highest environmental award and it was well deserved. Indeed, evidence of recycling is seen everywhere in the creative use of repurposed materials.

The bathrooms are uniquely decorated to look more like luxury spas than communal campground facilities, but all incorporate reclaimed

materials. Hand soap, hand towels, and bath mats make the spaces feel more homey and, as in most New Zealand campgrounds, there is a plug-in hair dryer on the counter ready for use. At the dump station, we laughed at the hose holder

made out of an old metal hospital bedpan.

Despite continued predictions about an approaching typhoon, we woke the next morning to a cloudy, but dry, day. The weather was perfect for a cruise on Lake Wakatipu that had been recommended by a friend. After purchasing tickets in the campground office, we made our way to the waterfront dock to board the coal powered steamer, the *TSS Earnslaw*. First launched in 1912, and now carefully restored, the ship is a fascinating reminder of a past era. Even 100 years later, its stately shape evokes visions of elegant travel. We were early enough to see the boat arrive from the previous cruise and watch as young deckhands shoveled coal on board.

The boat cruised along the lake, taking us to the *Walter Peak High Country Farm*, a working sheep station. Once on the boat, we found seats in the stern where we could watch the passing scenery. A pianist played and we relaxed as we enjoyed this bygone mode of transportation. We forayed to the front of the boat to watch coal being fed into the engines and observed how the engine works. This was interesting, especially to our mechanically minded guys.

We arrived at the *Walter Peak* farm just in time for lunch at the elegant homestead. A delicious barbecue of beef, lamb, and pork ribs was accompanied by tasty salads and desserts served in the gracious dining rooms. Next we watched a dog round up sheep from the pasture and corral them in a pen in front of us. This highly trained dog made it look easy and she seemed to enjoy the process. In fact, she looked disappointed to have to let the sheep go at the end. We loved getting to reach out and pat the puppies in a pen nearby.

Moving to an indoor shed, we watched a sheep shearing demonstration. As soon as the sheep is put onto its back, it stops struggling and is quite docile while its coat is removed. Amazing! The wool comes off in one big piece and, as soon as the shearing is completed, the sheep jumps up and runs off to join the rest of the herd. Next, we watched as the wool

was carded and spun into yarn on a large spinning wheel.

There was time to wander around the farm and enjoy the colorful gardens and the tranquil setting before it was time to board the ship for

the return to Queenstown. On the way back, the pianist played favorite New Zealand songs and we all joined in singing, thanks to the printed song sheets. What a great time we had!

On solid ground in Queenstown once more, the *Skyline Gondola*, the steepest cable car lift in the Southern Hemisphere drew our attention. The gondola to Bob's Peak climbs almost 1,500 feet above Queenstown and Lake Wakatipu. Once on top of the peak, we spent additional time enjoying the 220-degree vistas from the viewing terraces.

The Lynns opted for a Luge ride down the specially constructed track, a short walk from the top of the gondola. The Karpiseks watched from one of the observation platforms and cheered them on. Soon after, we headed back to town and the rain, which previously only threatened, began to pour down.

The rain tapered off during the night and morning brought sunny skies laced with fluffy white clouds. It looked good enough to allow us to go to Glenorchy, gateway to the New Zealand wilderness, where *Lord of the Rings, The Chronicles of Narnia, The Lovely Bones, The Hobbit,* and *X-Men Origins:*

Wolverines were filmed. The drive along the lake was enchanting and we stopped at several pull offs to view the changing colors of the water and billowing cloud formations.

Originally, we had considered taking a jet boat ride on the Dart River, but the weather was again threatening and the high cost of the ride deterred us. Instead, we walked around the docks and enjoyed a picnic by the lake. We strolled along a small tranquil stream feeling alone, far from the crowds of Queenstown. However, the spell was broken when a number of horse-back riders clomped through and the horses left evidence of their passing.

Exploring some of the backcountry roads outside of Glenorchy was fascinating and eerie. Mounded hills rose in front of jagged peaks and the river spread out in undulating curves. Low hanging greenery made us feel as if we had stepped into the forest primeval or at least a scene from *Lord of the Rings*.

The long awaited typhoon finally arrived as we were driving back to Queenstown. With night approaching and rain pelting down, one of the

Lynns' windshield wipers fell off, sailing into the bushes. *Really bad timing!* After a wet, fruitless search, we headed for an auto parts store, getting there just at closing time. With a new wiper installed and much better visibility, we pulled into our campsite with relief. (As instructed by *JUCY*, the Lynns saved the receipt and were reimbursed when they checked out at the end of the trip.) Thankfully, we did not let threats of a storm keep us from experiencing Glenorchy and, by the time the typhoon hit in full force, we were almost back to the campground.

Tips

- If you stay at the *Queenstown Top 10 Holiday Park Creeksyde*, be sure to walk around the campground and see all of the repurposed materials. Advanced reservations recommended for this campground.

- New Zealand is renowned for its sheep and the *Walter Peak High Country Farm*, via the *TSS Earnslaw*, is a good place to see a sheep station in operation.

- Even in the rain, the *Skyline Gondola* to Bob's Peak is worth doing.

- Check with campground offices if you want to purchase tickets for activities. Often, they will have them available on site, or, if they do not sell them, they can tell you the best place to go to obtain them.

High, Low and In-Between

QUEENSTOWN TO WESTPORT

Morning dawned bright and clear and our spirits rose with the prospect of a sunny day. Bill's priority was to take a jet boat ride and, since the Dart River hadn't worked out, we were curious to check out the famous jet boats on the Shotover River. However, though the ride looked exciting, it was not exactly what Bill was seeking. He wanted to actually see more of the river from the jet boat rather than have a short thrill ride, so once again we postponed that for later.

Arrowtown, an old gold mining site now primarily a tourist town, was next. Located on the tree-shaded gently flowing Arrow River, it is intriguing and the rustic main street invited us to browse in the unique shops and galleries and relax over lunch. We enhanced our picnic lunch with dessert from the local yogurt shop.

The settlement, where Chinese miners lived from 1865 to 1928, is located at the end of the main street. Brought in to work in the goldfields when the original miners left for richer fields, the Chinese miners came to earn money to support their families back home. They formed their own community apart from the rest of Arrowtown.

By 1874, there were 3,564 Chinese living in small huts made of mud brick, stone, wood, corrugated iron, and canvas and some of these have been partially restored. Thousands of miles from home, alone without their families, and crowded into substandard living quarters, the miners made the best of these dismal circumstances. Despite all the hardships, however, most never returned to China. Instead they settled in and became a part of the fabric of the community. Arrowtown is definitely a worthwhile stop with a look into New Zealand's past and the gold mining mania that swept the country.

Leaving Arrowtown, we drove over the Crown Range Road, a steep treeless pass and the highest main road in New Zealand. Although this is the shortest distance to Wanaka, it takes more time than the alternative route through Cromwell. Wanaka, located on Wanaka Lake, is surrounded by mountains. This small town seems laid back, but offers many of the same activities as the more touristy Queenstown. On this warm sunny day, many people were out enjoying the beach: sunbathing, floating in plastic rafts, and paddling rental kayaks. It looked like fun, but we needed to find a campground so we left the busy resort and found the *Wanaka Lakeview Holiday Park*, located near a quiet stretch of the lake. The tranquility of our large, shaded sites and the nearby deserted beach, provided the ideal place to unwind after our drive.

Realizing that our month was half over and we had a lot more to see, we elected to leave the warm summerlike beaches of Wanaka to head north. We were excited to drive over Haast Pass, labeled by guidebooks as one of the most scenic routes in the country. The ninety-mile drive, supposedly 2 1/2 to 3 hours, actually took most of the day. One reason was because we stopped so frequently to take photos. (We found out later that we were lucky to have made it over the pass when we did, because soon after it was closed by a rockslide.)

Looking down at a secluded cove on Lake Hawea and then crossing over to look out again at Lake Wanaka, each turn was more spectacular than the last. We followed a narrow river gorge punctuated by occasional waterfalls descending from great heights. Stopping to walk to *Thunder Creek Falls*, not too far off the road, was fun.

Lunch started outside at a picnic table overlooking the river valley, but we quickly fled back to our vans to escape the pesky little sandflies. Inside, we enjoyed the view, but without unwanted company. Finally reaching the other side of the pass, we stopped at the *Haast Visitor Centre* and browsed the displays of local plants, animals, and geological formations while talking to the ranger on duty.

The *Haast Beach Holiday Park* was an older, but nice campground. Rain and the persistent sandflies discouraged us from taking a hike on one of the nearby trails. When we arrived, we appeared to have the campground to ourselves, but as we were enjoying the kitchen and watching the evening news on TV, a group from Germany arrived and quickly and efficiently started to cook their evening meal. We briefly compared notes with them, but our dinner was ready and we sat down to eat while the others continued their meal preparations.

After dinner, we retreated to our campers to catch up on our journals and check our guidebooks for what lay ahead. In the morning, we enjoyed meeting a couple and their two children who had driven their large camper overland through Europe and China en route to Australia and New Zealand.

They planned to finish by driving across the United States and Canada. Wow! Hearing that they planned to be on the road for two years made our trip seem like a quick jaunt.

Leaving the campground, we paused for a quick look at a driftwood-covered beach on the Tasman Sea. Continuing on, we felt like we were driving along the Oregon Coast with views down to a wild ocean, diverse rock formations, and lonely stretches of beach. Along the way, the continuously changing scenery held our attention as we gazed at lush rainforests with numerous bridges over beautiful isolated rivers.

We noticed *Moeraki Lake* on our map and, using our walkie-talkies, agreed to take a lunch break there. While Bob fished, the rest of us relaxed in the light breeze that kept the sandflies at bay. The water was cold, but clear, and we were entertained by watching several bicyclists jump in the lake to cool off after their strenuous rides.

That afternoon we arrived at the modern *Fox Glacier Top 10 Campground*. It quickly filled up by dinnertime as this is a major stop on most tourists' itineraries.

After checking in, we piled into the Lynns' van to find the *Fox Glacier* trail with the goal of seeing the glacier up close. We walked beside the fast-moving glacier-silted river that nestled between towering rock walls. The last part of the trail was a bit steep, but worth the effort when we saw the glacier. That evening, we were treated to spectacular views of the sunset reflecting on the glaciers that rise above the nearby mountains.

In the morning, we woke to the sound of helicopters. Many visitors elect to view the glacier via helicopter so they can actually get out and walk on the ice. Since the weather was fantastic, the possibility of taking the ride and seeing glaciers from overhead was tempting. However, we agreed this was an unnecessary expense as we had all walked on a glacier in Canada. We elected, instead, to drive about two miles west to a location that had a terrific view. It was well worth it. What was amazing to us was that we were only a few miles from the ocean, but the mountains and glaciers were so close by.

Bypassing the *Franz Joseph* glacier, we made a brief stop in town for gas. Talking to a couple driving another *JUCY* at the gas station gave us an idea of where we wanted to stop that day. It was a long and tiring drive to Hokitika, but we made it and got campsites at the *Shining Star Beachfront Accommo-*

dation - *Caravan Park* that had been recommended to us by our *JUCY* acquaintances. The campground, located on the Tasman Sea, has a trail leading directly to the beach. The wide stretch of sand invited us to walk and the rocks provided comfortable seating for enjoying the view.

After dinner, we crossed the main road to see the glow-worm grotto that we had heard about. We felt quite adventur-

ous as we walked a short way up a dark path, trying not to use our flashlights or make any noise. As we reached the grotto, a glow of tiny white "Christmas lights" greeted us. It was enchanting to be in this silent forest, all alone, and surrounded by the twinkling lights. This small roadside grotto, largely bypassed by tourists, gave us the unique opportunity of seeing glowworms in a natural, outdoor, non-commercial setting.

In the morning, once again driving north along the coast on Route 6, we set our sights for a stop at *Punakaiki (PancakeRocks.)* After driving for miles without any traffic, we parked amidst many buses and joined all the people enjoying the view. This unique formation of layered limestone rocks, resembling stacks of pancakes, was unusual. A path winds around permitting the rocks to be viewed from many perspectives. Watching the tide surge into the large blowhole is fascinating.

Following the advice of a shopkeeper regarding where to find a good fishing spot, we drove about 1/4 mile back south the way we had come.

We turned onto a dirt road that was accessible to the public and stopped at a small car park. Bob went fishing while Joanne and Bill went exploring, following a trail that took them across a swing bridge, over the river, and back into the lush and serene forest. Marian relaxed with a book and was entertained by a friendly kea that kept coming out to see what was going on.

Moving on to Charleston, an old gold mining town, we elected to spend the night at the *Charleston Holiday Park & Motor Camp* because it was near the train we

wanted to take the next day. Our spaces were quiet and pleasant. New owners are working hard to update the facilities.

In the morning we found the *Charleston Nile River Rainforest Train* station and boarded the one-of-a-kind homemade train to see the jungle up close. The primary purpose of the train is to take cave trekkers to their starting point on the river, but other passengers may ride along. The tracks follow a stream up into the scenic mountain rain forest providing a glimpse of unspoiled New Zealand.

When we got to the end of the line, we meandered across a suspension bridge high over the glittering Nile River, watching trout dart about in the shadows beneath. The cavers, carrying large inner tubes, got off here and disappeared into the rainforest to climb up to the cave entrance.

We stayed on the train for the return journey. Leaving the train behind, we found the Charleston Reserve, located between Constant and Joyce Bays, where we had lunch and checked out the beach.

Continuing on, we drove over many one-lane bridges and finally came to open farm-land and more houses as we approached the city of West-port, our first large city since leaving Wanaka. We found the *Seal Colony Top 10 Holiday Park* directly across the street from the beach. Popular with surfers, its firm sand invited us to take a long walk that afternoon.

Tips

- Allow more time for driving than recommended in guidebooks.

- The glowworm grotto in Hokitika, across the street from the *Shining Star Beachfront Accommodation – Caravan Park* is magical at night.

- Camaraderie with campers, driving the same type van as you, can result in stimulating conversations and sightseeing tips.

River Fun

WESTPORT TO RICHMOND
The Karpiseks' Journey
BY MARIAN

When we were on the train the previous day, Bob talked to the "conductor" about good fishing spots nearby and received three recommendations of streams. Leaving Westport, we followed the directions and turned off Route 6 onto Route 65, a paved secondary road. The first location we found did not have good parking, the second looked difficult to fish, and access to the third was barred by an electric fence! Were we going to be thwarted trying to find a good fishing hole?

Although there was a fishing access sign posted on the fence, we were not comfortable opening the gate and driving onto private property. Just then we noticed a herd of over 100 cows slowly wending their way along a path just inside the fence. A woman on a four-wheeler cart followed the cows. Bob got out and talked to her and she graciously opened the gate to let us onto the land.

Following a good gravel road, we soon reached the burbling Mawherriti River. Bob immediately grabbed his fishing gear and strode upstream. I put out a chair and sat down to relax in the serene setting. Unfortunately, this magnificent place was also attractive to the ubiquitous sandflies and, despite applying copious amounts of insect repellent; the sandflies won the right to be outdoors. I grabbed my book and chair and dashed back to the van where I only had to contend with a few of the critters rather than the whole swarm.

When Bob returned after successfully catching and releasing several fish, we agreed that spending the night by the side of the stream as we originally planned was probably not going to be pleasant. So we packed up the van and left, being careful to secure the gate after we had passed through. Not too much further on, we came to Murchison where we decided to stop for the night. The *Murchison Kiwi Park Motels and Holiday Park*, a working farm, is a fun place. Emus, a wallaby, and a red deer roam the fields with chickens, ducks, and sheep. It was entertaining to watch as the campground host/ farmer fed them.

The clucking and quacking of early avian risers demanding to be fed woke us the next morning. After our own leisurely breakfast, we took to the road to find the *Richmond Motel and Top 10 Holiday Park* where we had arranged to meet Joanne and Bill. Although they had gone out for the day, we found their doormat in the space next to ours so we knew we were in the right place.

We spent the afternoon exploring the town of Richmond with its wide streets and plentiful parking. After window–shopping and strolling through the mall, we discovered the *Poppy Thai* restaurant which turned out to be a good choice for dinner. Traffic was so light that I felt very comfortable driving the van for the first time as we headed back to the campground. Richmond had another attribute we loved—we didn't see a sandfly and, indeed, we did not see any more during our time in New Zealand.

The Lynns' Journey

BY JOANNE

It was a gorgeous day when Bill and I left Westport heading east and then north to Richmond. At our Westport campground, we had picked up an advertisement for a jet boat ride and decided to call ahead to make sure there were tickets available. *Buller Gorge Swingbridge Adventure and Heritage Park* is a commercial operation with a high suspension swing bridge over the Buller River, the longest such bridge in New Zealand.

Visitors can hike on nature trails, picnic, skim through the air on zip lines, and pan for gold. Paying the fee for the jet boat allowed us to cross

the swingbridge where we enjoyed looking down on the water below—a fun stop in itself. We could see the boat at a dock on the other side.

This fit Bill's criteria exactly: a chance to see more miles of river and at a more reasonable cost than the prices we had seen in Queenstown. Finally, one of Bill's New Zealand "bucket list" items could be checked off!

We enjoyed having the opportunity to learn more about this river and the time to appreciate its beauty while moving downstream. Our driver even stopped to put the bow of the boat under a small waterfall for a few minutes. There were thrills too. Going at high speed, we would suddenly spin around with the ensuing spray almost engulfing us. Even though we were warned to hang on tightly to the bar in front of us, the force of the spin took me by surprise and I went sliding along the seat, with my husband and the driver grabbing me to keep me in place. These little jet boats can spin quickly!

Leaving the river behind, we drove through the small town of Murchison where fields of grazing cattle were surrounded by mountains. "This

reminds me of Wyoming!" Bill said as we picnicked in the park. Continuing on, we wound our way through forested mountains and down to Richmond, on the south side of Nelson, where we would eventually meet up with the Karpiseks. Our campground was comfortable, with all the amenities we were used to, but we missed being surrounded by nature.

We awoke to a grey, rainy day, but eager to see more, we decided to go into Nelson, one of the oldest New Zealand cities and a thriving arts center. Finding our way to the Nelson beach, located on Tasman Bay, we stopped to walk on the expanse of firm sand left by the low tide, and were amazed at the extreme tidal fluctuation.

Lured by a description of the coastal paradise of *Abel Tasman National Park*, we set our sights on the community of Kaiteriteri, only an hour to the west. When we finally glimpsed the beach, we were thrilled to see that the Caribbean-like turquoise water matched the description in our brochure. Best of all, the sun came out and invited us to put on our bathing suits and sit on the sand.

Surprisingly, when I put my feet into the water, it felt warm enough to swim in. While I investigated this inviting cove, Bill got out his chair and happily took in the sights while soaking up the sun and visiting with the couple whose van was parked next to ours.

When I saw three boats pulled up on the beach, I was intrigued to see what lay around the next corner. After talking with the captains, we opted

to take the "Coffee" cruise. This took us into another bay where we anchored and were served coffee and tea, and then went for a swim. While we enjoyed the drinks, our captain shared a glimpse of his world with us.

Our afternoon ended with a delightful, unexpected, piano recital by a young man who took a piano out of his van, rolled it out onto the beach, and started playing! What we saw and learned made us wish we had had the foresight to camp here (although the campground looked full.) Someday we would like to come back to kayak and have the water taxi drop us off at another cove for the day.

Tearing ourselves away, we searched for a place to grab some dinner (fish and chips) before driving back to Richmond. Reuniting with Marian and Bob, we wished we could have shared our experience with them. However, they had been off enjoying their own activities, so it was fun to share.

Tips

- Fishing on private property is allowed when posted on a fence or gate. If it is not posted, getting permission from the landowner is essential.

- If you open a gate, be sure to close it.

- Local maps of fishing access can be obtained from sporting goods stores.

- Call ahead to the *Buller Gorge Swingbridge Adventure and Heritage Park* if you want to be sure to have this jet boat experience.

- Reservations are recommended for camping at Kaiteriteri.

Farewell to the South Island

RICHMOND TO WELLINGTON

Enjoying the warmth of the sun and the promise of good weather, we set off for Picton where the ferry to Wellington and the North Island is

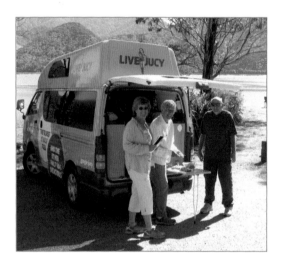

located. Stopping for lunch at Cable Bay we were fortunate enough to find a picnic table with a fantastic view. Here, just before Havelock, we had to choose whether to follow the coastline on the northern road, which the Lynns opted to do, or the southern road through the fabled wine country, which the Karpiseks selected.

The Lynns Take the Marlborough Sounds Route

BY JOANNE

Queen Charlotte Drive has been likened to cruising the Marlborough Sounds on land. The road is narrow and twisty, but the views are spectacular and there are plenty of places to pull out to admire the scenery. Each bay where boats bobbed at anchor in the sparkling blue-green water enticed us to take a picture. As Picton Harbor came into view, Bill and I were surprised to see that we were already at the end of the road.

The Karpiseks Take the "Wine" Route

BY MARIAN

Unlike the northerly Queen Charlotte Drive, the southern route is quite wide and straight. It goes through the famous Marlborough wine country where about 62% of all New Zealand wines are produced. Vineyards stretch on either side of the road as far as the eye can see and the land is lush and green. Although wine-tasting tours are readily available, Bob and I decided to forego this activity; just appreciating the beauty all around us was enough. We arrived in Picton ahead of the Lynns because we did not stop as often and our drive, although longer, was easier.

PICTON

Soon we were all together and checked into the *Picton Campervan Park*, a *Kiwi Holiday Park*. Lovely and tree-shaded, it was in walking distance of a small store and the harbour. A slight drawback to this campground, which was exceptionally clean and well maintained, was the low rumble of trucks passing every few hours during the night. We later learned that ferries operate 24 hours a day and offload commercial trucks every two or three hours. No wonder it was a little noisy, but we slept well in spite of that. The proximity to the harbor and the ferry more than made up for the minor disruption.

We set out to look around the town and find the ferry that would take us to Wellington the next day. The wharf at Picton is colorfully iconic and we saw all sizes and shapes of boats tied up to the docks. Thankfully, there was no cruise ship visiting the port that day.

The public restroom at the wharf is one of the most interesting "activities" in Picton! A green light indicates when the facility is available. The door swings open when a button is pressed. Inside, a disembodied voice from the ceiling intones "press the button to lock the door" and "you have ten minutes." Lovely music plays. Toilet paper is released with the push of a button, but there is no button to push to flush. However, a sign states that the toilet will flush when hands are washed or when the cubicle is exited. We all agreed we had never seen such a sophisticated, practical public bathroom, and each of us had to have a turn to see it for ourselves.

The next morning we took another walk around the harbor and then a brief drive to a lookout where we could enjoy the bustling waterfront scene below. By then it was time to line up at the *Interislander Ferry Terminal* for our crossing. We passed the time waiting in line by having lunch and sitting outside watching the other vehicles prepare to load. We drove onto the ferry along with another *JUCY* van. Our three campers

were dwarfed by the trucks surrounding them. (Later, we noticed people taking pictures of the vans nestled among the big rigs.)

Leaving the vans as required, we took an elevator to the tenth deck where we sat outside and watched the sun sparkling on Picton as it slowly disappeared in the distance. Our journey to the North Island had begun. We had been a bit worried about this three-hour crossing having read descriptions of heavy, stormy seas that sometimes prevail in the Cook Strait. Bill put on a patch to prevent seasickness, but the water was as smooth as glass and the patch was unnecessary.

What a great day to be out on the water! When the guys got tired of sitting out on deck, they went inside where comfortable chairs in front of a big picture window enticed them to settle in for a nap. Staying outside, we were watching the passing scenery when suddenly someone yelled "dolphins!" We rushed to watch a pod of dolphins surfing playfully in the ship's wake.

Finally we also moved inside and found a table where we could read and plan the next phase of our journey. The South Island had more than met our expectations and we eagerly anticipated what we would find on the North Island. With so much to do on this last leg, we would have to budget our time carefully to make the most of the eight days we had left.

Tips

- Make ferry reservations ahead of time to ensure getting the time you want.

- Take precautions for seasickness, if necessary, so you can enjoy the ferry.

- It's possible to sit inside by a window for the entire time, but you will see things from the outer decks that you will miss if you stay inside.

- Snacks and drinks are available on the ship.

- If crowds are a problem for you, try to select a date to arrive in Picton when a cruise ship is not in port.

Captivated by Worms

WELLINGTON TO WAITOMO

The capital city of Wellington, with a population of over 396,000 people, is the second-largest city in New Zealand. Modern, with many cafes and restaurants, it is located around Fitzroy Bay and has a vibrant waterfront. As we drove off the ferry in Wellington, we realized that we were arriving exactly at rush hour and the congested ferry parking lot exited onto a very busy road.

With relief, we spotted Joanne's friend, Steve, who was looking for us, unsuccessfully waving at two other *JUCY*s that came off before us. Steve, a family friend of the Lynns, whom Joanne first met when he came to California as a high school exchange student, lives and works in a community outside of Wellington.

Thankfully we could follow him instead of negotiating the traffic on our own. Steve led us up a very narrow, winding road that ended at *Mt. Victoria*, a glorious lookout with 360-degree views of the city and harbor. He pointed out various points of interest and we enjoyed this personal introduction to the North Island, relishing the changing colors as the sun set on the city. Great planning on Steve's part as we purposely took our time, waiting for rush hour traffic to end before resuming our tour.

Back down to the city, we were excited to find three adjacent parking spaces right where we wanted to be. We visited the historic *Embassy Theater* where *The Hobbit* film premiered. Peter Jackson, director of the Hobbit films and a Wellington native, donated artifacts and memorabilia to recreate the ambiance of "Middle Earth" in the theater.

After our immersion in the Hobbit world, we walked to the *Masala* restaurant for dinner. The prices are reasonable and the curries excellent. Caravanning back to Steve's home, we had a quick cup of tea and then "freedom camped" in his driveway.

After coffee and toast with Steve in the morning, we talked until it was time for him to leave for work. This visit was special, as Joanne enjoyed reconnecting with Steve and all of us learned more about living in New Zealand from the perspective of a resident. We wanted to stay longer, but

Steve helped us clarify distances and priorities for the short time we had left and we knew we needed to drive on.

After a quick stop at the supermarket, we took off. Even with the GPS, we got a little lost making our way out of town while skirting a lake and estuary, but finally reached Route 1. After a fairly easy drive, we stopped for lunch at the wild and deserted beach of Te Horo. We had fun skipping rocks and looking for shells.

In the late afternoon, we decided we had driven far enough and *Whanganui River Top 10 Holiday Park* was nearby. This is a huge park, but because it was off-season, there were only a few other campers. Paying a little extra for a spot right on the river, we enjoyed watching boaters and being entertained by a friendly goat grazing ten feet away. The goat doubled as a lawn mower and playmate for children.

The Whanganui River, listed as a national canoe trail, caught the eye of Joanne and Bill. Here in the valley the river flows gently and is wide enough for rowing crews to practice, but we were a little disappointed by the muddy color. Still it was fun to think about the possibility of returning some day for a multi-day canoe trip.

After a breakfast of scrambled eggs and English muffins, cooked in the large camper kitchen, we were back on the road again. Route 4 was country driving at its best—wider and with beautiful scenery. We observed that the North Island is quite different from the South Island; it is hillier, rockier and drier. As we followed a canyon, snaking its way along below us, we stopped to walk out on a single-lane bridge over a stream. Peering down, hoping to spot some trout, we instead saw quite a few geese paddling slowly by.

In Te Kuiti, we saw crowds of people, some carrying chairs as if going to a parade. Curiosity got the better of us and we stopped to ask what was going on. We learned that everyone was out to see the old steam engine train that only operates from Auckland to Te Kuiti once a year. Just then, we saw plumes of black smoke coming our way and we jumped out to  take a picture. What a fortunate coincidence for us!

We arrived at the *Waitomo Top 10 Holiday Park*, our headquarters for exploring the glowworm caves. Discussing options with the campground hosts, we decided against the most popular forty-five minute tour taken by most groups. Instead, we selected more in-depth experiences and booked our tickets for the next day.

This campground is a busy place with a nice swimming pool and Jacuzzi, which we enjoyed after the long driving day. We could walk to a restaurant and café across the street if we were so inclined, but since we had plenty of food with us, picnicking allowed us to enjoy the delightful warm evening instead.

The Lynns' Black Water Rafting Tour

BY JOANNE

Excited and a little apprehensive about the physical requirements of our tour (Bill had hip replacement surgery the year before) we drove two miles to the *Black Water Rafting Company* headquarters. Located in a modern building, complete with a souvenir shop and cafe, the staff answered our questions as we waited for our group to be called.

Looking around, we realized we were decisively the oldest participants as the other members of our group appeared to be college age. However, we reminded ourselves, we lead yearly rafting trips and often hike in the mountains so are very fit for our age. Our guide briefed us about the itin-

erary and ushered us into a changing area to don excruciatingly wet, cold, and clumsy wet suits, bootie socks, and rubber boots.

As soon as we each had a helmet with a headlamp, we all jumped into a van for the short drive to the car park near the cave entrance. There, we were given large inner tubes and practiced how to sit in them and raft up in a single line. After a talk on how to jump in backwards, I was selected to demonstrate first, jumping off and down into the stream. "Ohhh its cold!" I screamed, as I bounced around, splashing to keep my balance. Being first allowed me to laugh as each of the others were shocked by the cold water.

Hoisting the large tubes over our shoulders, we followed our guide up a quarter-mile path to the cave entrance. This was the most difficult part for me as I struggled, a little out of breath, to keep up with the young folks.

Entering the cave at last, through a narrow entrance, we sat down in the dark cavern and, with only our headlamps for light, learned about the history of the cave. After that, for at least an hour, we alternately walked and waded through shallow water, before coming to a section where we could float along on our tubes. It was very dark. Several times we came to a drop off and had to jump three to four feet backwards down to the next level. A bit scary, but thrilling and exciting!

We paused and gathered at a wider spot to rest up, eat the snack the guides provided, and warm our hands a little. Then we entered a long tunnel-like section of the cave. We turned off our lights and, rafting up, were thrilled to see the little starry lights created by the glowworms. Silently we floated, pushing our way along in the dark with our hands on the narrow rock walls.

Afterward, warming up over cups of hot tomato soup, we watched the pictures our guide took of us with her *GoPro* camera, and ordered a copy for ourselves to preserve this memory. This was an indescribably awesome, physical, adrenalin-filled adventure and definitely one that is a highlight of our lives. We're so glad we did not chicken out. This is one activity to do before you have mobility issues. Bill, by the way, had no trouble at all keeping up!!

The Karpiseks' "Spellbound" Tour

BY MARIAN

Half an hour after the Lynns left, Bob and I walked across the street from the campground to the *Spellbound Glowworm and Cave Tour* office. We checked in and Norm, our guide, loaded our group into a van for the twenty-minute drive to the sheep and cattle farm where our first cave was located. Waitomo is located on top of a limestone formation created over a period of five million years. The *Spellbound Glowworm Cave*, part of the Mangawhitkau cave system, has been featured in several BBC productions, including "Planet Earth."

Climbing out of the van, we walked a short distance through limestone outcroppings down to a picturesque little stream. There we donned our hard hats and crossed a small bridge, as we walked to the cave entrance.

Inside, with the only illumination coming from our headlamps, we were fascinated as we made our way deeper and deeper into

Photo courtesy of Spellbound Glowworm and Cave Tour.

the darkness beside the gently flowing stream. We shortly came to a dock where a small rubber raft was tied. Climbing in, we turned off our lights.

There is no way to adequately describe the feeling of floating on dark, silky water surrounded by 30,000 twinkling fairy lights. It is magical and mystical; like being part of the Milky Way or looking at another universe. No one spoke a word as we sat enchanted by the spell of the glowworms.

Eventually, we had to return to the dock and reality. As we left the cave, we couldn't believe the number of glowworms that we noticed in places where we hadn't seen them before. Our eyes had become more attuned to our surroundings after being in the dark.

Turning in our hard hats, we walked across a field to a shed where Norm prepared a snack for us. Coffee, tea, and cocoa with biscuits were a welcome treat. After a brief rest, we set off for a second cave.

The "Cave of the Spirit" (Te Ana o te Atua) was known to the ancient Maori who often stopped to visit it; in fact, one of their walking trails wends its way past the cave. This was the first New Zealand cave explored and recorded by a European, Dr. Arthur Thompson, in 1849. It is a dry cave with stalactites and stalagmites, columns, and flow formations. The rock was originally white but, due to an ancient flood, some of the oldest rocks are now brown.

The highlight of this cave was a complete moa skeleton. Moas, large flightless birds native to New Zealand, were an easy food source for the Polynesians who first populated the island. Unfortunately, because moas were easily hunted, they became extinct about 1400. This cave, at one time, contained many moa bones, but most were removed by early visitors. We were privileged to see the one remaining skeleton.

The *Spellbound* cave tour lived up to and surpassed our expectations. We were indeed, spellbound, and this was a highlight not only of our New Zealand trip, but one of the most memorable experiences in all of our many travels.

Tips

- Avoid arriving in Wellington during rush hour if at all possible.

- You may want to allow more time for the North Island than we did. Two weeks would have been better.

- If you don't have reservations in popular tourist areas, plan to arrive early in the day.

- Waitomo is a "must see" location.

- Choose a glowworm tour that matches your fitness and interest level.

Maoris and More

ROTORUA TO AUCKLAND

We met up again after our Waitomo tours, excited to share the highlights of what we had seen and done. Now it was time to investigate Rotorua. The drive was surprisingly easy and, after reading our brochures, we decided to check out the *Waiteti Trout Stream Holiday Park.* Driving past warehouses, it looked like this might not be a good choice, but a quick peek inside the grounds convinced us that this was where we wanted to camp. Bob, of course, was delighted at the prospect of trout fishing.

A stream, home to some black swans and their cygnets, meandered past our campsites. We knew we had made the right choice when we walked down a shaded path, glorious with flowers and other greenery, to Lake

Rotorua. It was like being inside a Monet painting. As the use of kayaks was included in the campground fee, Joanne jumped into one to take a closer look.

The next day Bob was up early to fish while the rest of us went into Rotorua to learn more about the Maori. Our first stop was the *Rotorua Museum*, located in the old bath house where, for many years, New Zealanders vacationed at the thermal spas. While watching a film on the history of Rotorua, we were startled when our seats suddenly began to shake as the film recreated an earthquake like the one caused by the Tarawera eruption that destroyed much of the region in 1886 and dramatically altered the land. Many of the exhibits in the museum relate to Maori history, culture, legends and stories. A Maori canoe and other artifacts make visiting this museum worthwhile.

Next, we took a guided tour of *Whakarewarewa Thermal Village* whose actual name is *Tewhakarewarewatangaoteopetauaawahiao.* Try

saying that! This old Maori village is still in use today and we learned how the Maori incorporate the hot springs into their daily lives. Long before we were using slow cookers, they were making their meals in the steam from the geysers and simmering food in thermal pools. We laughed as our guide told us that she sometimes cooks her TV dinner this way. Baths, carved from the indigenous stone and filled with water from the thermal springs, create a place for the residents to luxuriate in the warm water.

Back in the campground, we found Bob ecstatic at having caught (and released) three fish while we were gone. We all felt our day had been well spent. Now it was time to get ready to take part in a cultural evening at the *Mitai Maori Village*. The activities would feature a hangi dinner, a traditional form of cooking. Transportation to the village was included in the cost of the evening so we did not have to move our vans or worry about driving at night.

After all buses arrived, we trekked out to where the meat was cooking in the hangi. The aroma of chicken, beef, and lamb roasting in the pit made us drool, but there was more to do before dinner time. First, we went to a small stream where chanting Maori warriors rowed past us in a canoe lit only by a flaming torch.

Aspects of the Maori culture were explained as we were treated to demonstrations of skills, weapons, fighting, housing, dancing, and instruments. An outdoor theater, in the bush, provides an ideal backdrop for these stories.

Finally, dinner was served in the big central building. The meats, succulent after roasting for hours in the hangi, were accompanied by many other delicious dishes and we ate with gusto. A lively emcee kept us entertained as he recognized and acknowledged the diverse audience that represented twenty different countries.

To end the evening, we were led on a short walk to a spring where we could see the clear, cold water bubbling up. The lights were turned off and a few glowworms shone in the dark. Many in the audience were impressed, but, to us, these few glow-worms seemed almost insignificant, although the overall ambiance was enchanting. We thoroughly enjoyed the informative and entertaining evening that gave us a deeper appreciation for the Maori and their way of life.

The next morning we decided that we needed to start our drive to Auckland. On reflection, we wished we had planned at least another day in Rotorua because there was so much to see and do, but we were fast running out of time. So, once again the open road beckoned.

We made a brief stop at *Okere Falls*, north of Rotorua, a popular spot for kayaking and rafting. A group of people were learning to kayak and it was fun watching them discover how to move into the river and navigate the cur-

rents. We wanted to linger longer, but needed to keep moving.

We decided to stop for the night when we reached the coast and the *Papamoa Beach Top 10 Holiday Resort*. We were given RV spaces on a hill overlooking the Pacific Ocean. The beach was littered with a wide array of shells of all sizes and a stroll along the edge of the water yielded more shells to add

to the collection we found in our campsite. It was a relaxing way to spend our last night before reaching the busy metropolis of Auckland.

Leaving vacation paradise behind, we reluctantly embarked on our last full driving day. We encountered trucks, traffic and construction that made driving difficult. Needing a break around noon, we turned off Route 2 onto a secondary road that led to *Miranda Hot Springs*. We had lunch in the parking lot and took a dip in the lovely warm mineral pool.

Reaching Auckland during rush hour was not a good plan. We had difficulty finding the *Manukau Holiday Park* where we had reservations to spend our last night. Our GPS, which was several years old, had been a big help, but in Auckland, it let us down. New roads had replaced old ones and the GPS didn't know this. However, by using the tried and true method of stopping and asking for directions, we finally arrived at the campground.

It was filled with others who, like us, were preparing to return their campers before going home. Our dinner that night consisted of "soup," made of a lot of leftover ingredients that used up many of our remaining supplies. Those that were left we added to the pile in the campground

kitchen. Newcomers to the island would find many items to stock their campers; indeed, no one would ever need to buy salt and pepper shakers as there must have been hundreds available!

The rest of the evening and the next morning saw us packing, giving away, throwing away and cleaning as we prepared to say good-bye to the vans that had been our homes for the last month. A late check-out gave us the time we needed and, finally, we were ready to return our vehicles and spend the rest of the day sightseeing in Auckland.

The *JUCY* rental office, located near the airport, was only minutes away, but finding it with our old GPS was difficult. Luckily, we spotted the bright green vans and were able to make our way there. Checking in was quick and efficient. In short order, we turned in our keys and were in a taxi heading to the Auckland wharf.

Rain was pelting down as our cab came to a stop and we darted across the street to the shelter of a restaurant where we had lunch. Our window seats allowed us to watch the activity on the boats moored nearby. Wanting to see more than the high rises of Auckland, we decided to take a small ferry to the community of Davenport, across the Waitemata Harbour.

The ten minute ride, filled with locals commuting from the city to the suburbs, offered panoramic views of Auckland and we could appreciate the city from this perspective. Enchanted by a breathtaking rainbow, we walked along the bay front and beach taking pictures, but the rain began again and we rushed to catch the next ferry back to the mainland.

On reaching the dock, we were amazed and pleased to find our taxi driver already waiting to take us back to the campground where we had left our luggage. Then it was on to the airport to board our return flight to Honolulu. It was with sadness that we bid farewell to New Zealand and the wonderful people and places we experienced. We couldn't believe that this trip, that we had planned for so long, was over. However, in reflecting on all we had done, we realized that each of us had fulfilled our original goal. Still there was so much left to see and do that we could have kept going for many more days.

The image lingering in our minds as we settled into our seats for the flight back to Honolulu was of the glorious rainbow we saw earlier in the day in Davenport. Every rainbow ends in a pot of gold, according to legend, and our own pot of gold is a treasure of New Zealand memories that we'll cherish forever.

Tips

- Campground reservations are recommended for large cities where many campers are beginning and ending their trips.

- Consider taking a taxi to sightsee in cities rather than trying to maneuver your camper van through heavy traffic and find parking.

- Be sure your GPS has current information

Information

CAMPER VAN
JUCY www.JUCY.co.nz/

CAMPGROUND SOURCES
(Brochures available free at campgrounds and rental agencies)

Top 10 Holiday Parks   www.top10.co.nz/

Kiwi Holiday Parks   www.kiwiholidayparks.com/

Jason's New Zealand Camping and Holiday Park Guide
    www.jasons.co.nz

Official Tourism Site for New Zealand
    www.newzealand.com/us/holiday-parks/

New Zealand Travel Reviews
    www.rankers.co.nz

Freedom Camping   www.tourism.net.nz

HELPFUL TOUR BOOKS
The Rough Guide to New Zealand
Lonely Planet New Zealand

FISHING INFORMATION
Fish and Game New Zealand Official Site   www.fishandgame.org.nz

New Zealand Freshwater Fishing   www.nzfishing.com

Sandfly Information
    www.goodbyesandfly.co.nz
    www.teara.govt.nz/en/sandflies-and-mosquitoes/page-1

Acknowledgements

Many thanks to Bob Karpisek and Bill Lynn for their driving skills that made this trip enjoyable and for their support and patience that made this book possible. Appreciation to Gary Lynn and Danielle Ciminero for their technical assistance. Special thanks to Maureen Arrigo for her careful editing and Sharyl Smith for her critiquing that helped make the finished product more exact and readable.

About the Authors

Joanne Lynn, a retired adapted physical education teacher, has spent much of her life traveling and camping. She has worked as a licensed white water rafting guide, swim instructor, and camp counselor. Her first van camping trip was seven weeks in Europe in 1970 just after she and her husband were married. She and Bill, have slept out under the stars and camped in a variety of different sized RVs. Currently they enjoy their truck camper which tows a jeep so they can enjoy exploring the western U.S.

Marian Karpisek has camped with her family, in all 48 of the continental states and most of Canada, in everything from a make-shift tent to a trailer to a motor home. Her first experience in a camper van was a month spent in Great Britain with her husband, Bob, in 1984. They spent six years living and traveling in their Class B motor home after she retired as a school library media supervisor. She is the author of two books and many articles on school libraries and travel.

Printed in Great Britain
by Amazon